How do I feel about

OUR

NEW

BABY

Jen Green

COPPER BEECH BOOKS • BROOKFIELD, CONNECTICUT

Designed and produced by
Aladdin Books Ltd
28 Percy Street
London W1P 0LD

First published in the United States
in 1998 by
Copper Beech Books,
an imprint of
The Millbrook Press
2 Old New Milford Road
Brookfield, Connecticut 06804

Printed in Belgium
5 4 3 2 1

Designer   Gary Edgar-Hyde
Editor   Sarah Levete
Illustrator   Christopher
                O'Neill
Photographer   Roger Vlitos

**Library of Congress
Cataloging-in-Publication Data**
Green, Jen.
Our new baby / Jen Green.
p. cm. — (How do I feel about)
Includes index.
Summary: Discusses the fun and frustration of coping
with being a big brother or sister to a new baby, the
disruption to the normal family life, and the sharing of
the parents' time, attention, and love.
ISBN 0-7613-0871-7 (lib. bdg.)
1. Infants—Juvenile literature.
2. Brothers and sisters—Juvenile literature.
[1. Babies. 2. Brothers and sisters.]
I. Title. II. Series.
HQ774.G725 1998   98-16958
306.875—dc21   CIP AC

Contents

Introduction

Dean, Rosie, Max, and May are in the same class at school. Dean's mom is expecting a new baby and so is Rosie's mom. New babies bring changes to any family. Dean, May, Max, and Rosie talk about what a new brother or sister will mean to them.

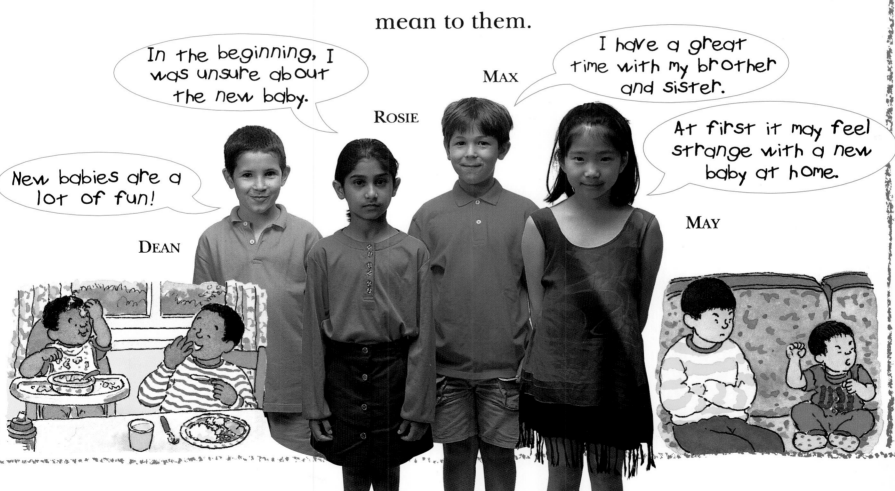

Expecting A Baby

Dean and Max are good friends at school. Dean has been looking forward to telling Max his news. Dean's mom is pregnant — she will be having a new baby. The baby will be born in five months' time. Dean is excited about having a new baby brother or sister to play with. Is a new baby expected in your family?

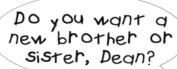

Do you want a new brother or sister, Dean?

Yeah. I'm really looking forward to it.

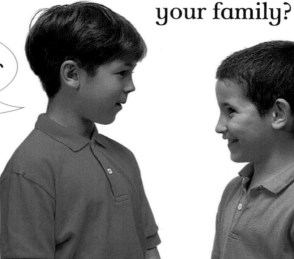

You can have fun in a small family...

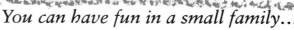

... or in a large family.

▽ Where Do Babies Come From?

All babies begin from a tiny egg and a seed, called a sperm. The egg comes from the mother. The sperm comes from the father. When they join together, a new baby begins inside the mother.

◁ How Babies Grow

A baby grows in the mother's womb near the stomach. At first the new baby is tiny, but slowly it gets bigger. The mother's tummy gets larger, too. If your mom is pregnant you may be able to feel the baby moving in her tummy.

Dean, how do you feel about the new baby?

"I'm really excited. I've already got a younger sister, Sonia. I was only three when she was born so I don't remember much about it. This time I'm going with Mom for her checkup. There's a special machine there that shows you the shape of the baby on a T.V. screen."

Mixed Feelings

Rosie lives with her mom and her stepdad, Steve. When Rosie went home with the news about Dean's family, Rosie's mom told her that she was also expecting a baby. Rosie says she has mixed feelings about it. Dean says that his little sister Sonia is also unhappy about the news. If a new baby is expected in your family, how do you feel about it?

You may feel happy ...

...or you may feel unhappy.

▽ *Stepfamilies*

If you live with only one of your parents, and your mom or dad is expecting a baby with a new partner, you might feel a bit left out. You might feel the new baby will get more love. But a new baby won't change your mom or dad's love for you. There will be enough love to go around for everyone.

Sorry, I'm too tired to play.

◁ *Pleased or Angry?*

When a baby is expected, you may feel excited or proud. But you may also feel bored or impatient if your mom is feeling tired. You might also feel angry if she can't play with you as much as she did before.

Why don't they want to see my picture?

▷ *How Your Mom Feels*

If your mom is expecting a baby, she may feel sick in the mornings. She may need more rest than usual. This is nothing to worry about. A growing baby uses up lots of your mom's energy. As the baby gets bigger, your mom may need help to lift heavy things.

7

Mixed Feelings

1. A new baby was due in Harry's family. Harry was worried about it.

2. Harry's dad realized Harry was upset. He asked him what was wrong.

3. Harry's dad said that Harry had an important part to play in the family.

Why was Harry feeling worried?

If a new baby is due in your family, it's natural to feel a bit anxious. Like Harry, you may feel pleased, but also wonder quite how things will be. Harry talked to his dad. His dad explained they were so happy with Harry that they decided to have a new baby, too.

If you feel worried, talk to your parents. Your mom and dad will understand how you feel.

▽ Getting Ready

There are many things to prepare for a new baby. The baby will need somewhere to sleep. You may have to move your things around, or move to a new room. Do you have any old toys that the new baby may like to play with?

Don't be sad about the new baby. It will all be Ok.

◁ All Change

A baby means change for everyone. You may find this easy or you may find it hard, and wish that things could stay the way they were. If you already have a little brother or sister, he or she might feel upset about no longer being the youngest child.

Are you looking forward to the new baby, Rosie?

"Yes and no. My mom and dad don't live together anymore. Now Mom and my stepdad, Steve, are having a new baby. I thought the new baby might be more special to them than me. But mom says that having a new baby won't change the way she feels about me."

The Birth

It's May's birthday today. Max is giving May a card and present to celebrate. May is now eight years old. Eight years ago today she was born in the hospital. May says she was born at nine o' clock in the morning. Do you know what happened when you were born? Where did it happen and who was there?

It's often a rush before the birth.

A birthday is a very special day.

▼ *In the Hospital*

After nine months in the mother's womb, the new baby is ready to be born. Your mom may go into the hospital to have her baby. Your dad may go with her. While the baby is being born, your parents will ask a relative or a close friend to come and look after you.

◄ *At Home*

Your mom may decide to have her baby at home. A midwife, who is a special person who helps to deliver a baby, may come to help your mom. Your mom and dad may also arrange for a relative or friend to take care of you for a short while.

► *How Long?*

A baby's birth may take only a few hours. Or it can take a full day. If your mom goes to the hospital to have her baby, she may be home a few hours after it is born. Or she may stay in the hospital for a few days. It's a big day when the baby comes home at last.

The Birth

1. Fred's mom was having a baby in the hospital. Fred's dad called to speak to him.

2. The next day Fred went to see his mom in the hospital. Fred's mom gave him a big hug.

3. Fred was excited when he saw the baby. His mom let Fred hold him for a while.

How did Fred feel about the birth of his baby brother?

Fred missed his mom when she was in the hospital, even though his favorite aunt looked after him. When his dad called to tell him about his new brother, Fred wasn't sure what he felt. But when he saw his mom, everything felt fine again. Don't worry if your mom goes away to have her baby. She and your dad will soon be home.

▼ Ready to Play?

You may want to play with your new brother or sister right away. But newborn babies don't play much at first. They mostly sleep and feed. But they do like to be held. Support the baby's head while you are holding him or her.

◀ Growing Up

Things change fast with a new baby. After three months the baby will be awake for longer, and will want you to play with him or her. Soon the baby will eat solid food. You might like to help with feeding — it may be messy!

May, do you know what happened when you were born?

"Yes, my mom told me. I was born in the hospital. Mom said it took sixteen hours for me to be born. She said she was very pleased when I arrived at last! I've got two younger sisters. They were both born at home. My youngest sister, Jo, only took four hours to be born."

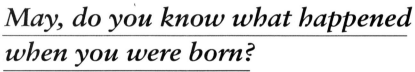

A Newborn Baby

Max's teacher asked everyone in the class to bring in photos of themselves as babies. They stuck the photos on the wall and guessed who was who. No one guessed which one was Max. Later Max and Rosie talked about babies. Do you know what you were like as a baby? Did you cry or sleep a lot?

Newborn babies are so small. I'd be scared to hold one.

Mom says you must hold them firmly but carefully.

A baby feeds from the mom's breast.

Or a baby feeds from a bottle.

▼ Playing With The Baby

Newborn babies are very small at first — but don't be scared to play with them! Babies like to look at people's faces. They learn to talk by copying the sounds we make so sing nursery rhymes and talk to the baby.

Make the baby laugh by being as silly as you like!

◀ Why Do Babies Cry?

Crying is a baby's only way of saying he or she needs something. A baby cries to get attention, if they are hungry or uncomfortable, or bored.

Don't feel upset if the baby cries. You may get really good at knowing what the baby wants.

▶ Sleeping Problems

New babies need to feed often, including at night. Your mom and dad will be tired if they get up several times at night.

You may also sleep badly, especially if you can hear the baby crying. There is nothing to worry about, so try to relax at night.

1. Sasha and her family were very excited. The new baby had just come home.

2. But when friends came over, the baby was the center of attention. Sasha felt left out.

3. Later Sasha talked it over with her mom.

Why was Sasha upset?

Sasha was really pleased about the new baby. But she got upset when she felt no one was paying any attention to her anymore. Things may feel different at first with a new baby at home. It will take time to get used to having a little stranger in the family. Talk things over with your mom and dad. Talking about your feelings nearly always helps.

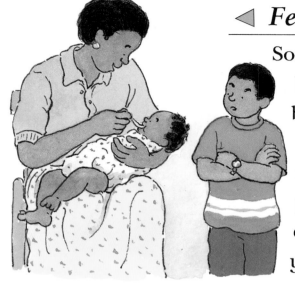

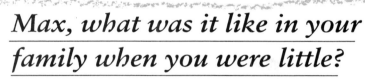

A Newborn Baby

▼ Good Times

You will probably have lots of different feelings about the baby. You may feel really pleased most of the time. You may love to play with the baby, and enjoy bathtimes or feeding. You may be best at making the baby laugh.

◀ Fed Up?

Sometimes you may feel bored or fed up about the baby. You may feel your mom and dad now have less time for you. Talk to your parents. Perhaps you can agree on a special time for you and your mom or dad.

Max, *what was it like in your family when you were little?*

"My older brother was eight and my sister was four when I was born. Mom said they helped a lot when I was little. They played with me and helped teach me to talk and to read. I learned to walk quickly so I could keep up with them!"

17

My New Brother Or Sister

May and Dean are showing each other pictures of the people in their families, which they drew at school. Dean said he and his sister, Sonia, play together a lot. May said she used to get along badly with her younger sister, Amy, but now they are good friends. If you've got brothers and sisters, how do you get along with them?

My sister Sonia is really good at making up games.

I get mad when Amy beats me at cards.

Some brothers and sisters get along.

18

Others seem to fight a lot.

▽ *Talking, Walking*

Of course, you can do hundreds of things a baby cannot do. Young babies cannot feed themselves or use a potty. But they grow up fast. At six months, a baby may start to crawl. At nine months, he or she may begin to say a few words.

◁ *Safety First*

Babies have no idea about what is safe. They put things into their mouths to taste them and to see if they are soft or hard. But you know what is not safe to eat, and places that aren't safe to go near. This can really help when you are keeping an eye on the baby.

▷ *Younger Brothers And Sisters*

If you have a younger brother or sister, he or she may not feel as you do about the baby. He or she is more likely to feel angry and a bit left out.

If you spend time with your little brother or sister, it can really help them to feel special, too.

19

1. Jack felt that his mom only ever played with his new sister. He felt angry and hit his mom.

2. Jack said his mom didn't care about him. Jack's mom said hitting wasn't allowed.

3. Next time he felt angry, Jack kicked a ball. After a while he felt a bit better.

Why did Jack feel angry?

With the new baby, Jack felt angry and left out. Like him, you might feel angry. After all, you didn't choose to have a new baby in your family. You may feel like breaking something or even hitting someone. But this would only make things worse. Talk about your feelings. If you still feel angry, hit something soft, like a cushion, or kick a ball outside.

20

▼ Family Fights

Sometimes you may quarrel with your brother or sister. But you probably stick up for each other when it matters most. Some brothers and sisters quarrel a lot when they are young, but become good friends later.

◀ Sharing

You may feel jealous of your brother or sister. You may find it hard to share your mom and dad.

But just because your parents love your new sister or brother, doesn't mean they will love you any less.

How do you get along with your sisters, May?

"Amy was born when I was three. I felt a bit jealous of her at first. Then, when I was six and Amy was three, Jo was born. I liked playing with Jo, but I could see Amy felt angry. I told Amy I knew how she was feeling. Now Amy and I play together a lot."

21

Don't Forget . . .

How do you feel now about the new baby in your family, Rosie?

"At first I didn't like the idea of lots of change. After Mom and I talked about it, I felt better. I talked things over with Steve, my stepdad. I'm looking forward to it now. I'm going to help choose the baby's name."

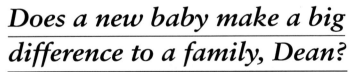

Does a new baby make a big difference to a family, Dean?

"You may feel as if you get your own way less when there is a new baby around. But no one gets their own way all the time. Having a new baby in our family helped me to see that other people's feelings were important too. It's good, too, because we can have lots of fun now that our family is bigger."

May, do you find it easy to talk things over in your family?

"When my sister Amy was small, for a while I thought that Mom and Dad loved her more than me. But I told Mom and Dad how I felt.

They said that they loved us both just as much, but sometimes Amy needed more looking after because she was a baby."

Do you like having a brother and sister, Max?

"Yeah. It's great. I learned from my big brother and sister. There's a video of my brother teaching me to walk. It's really funny. Now that I'm older, we all have even more fun together."

23

Index

All the photographs in this book have been posed by models. The publishers would like to thank them all.

Charlestown Branch Library
179 Main Street
Charlestown, MA 02129-3299